Hoole's Guide
to
British
Collecting
Clubs

©Les Hoole

First published in Great Britain in 1992 by
Adwalton Publishing
14 Penfield Road
Adwalton
Drighlington
Bradford
West Yorkshire BD11 1ES

Printed by
Thornton & Pearson (Printers) Ltd
Bradford

ISBN 0 9520690 0 8

British Library Cataloguing in Publication Data
A catalogue record of this book is available from the British Library

INTRODUCTION

Collecting is one of the worlds most popular hobbies. Perhaps nowhere more so than in Britain, the birthplace of the postage stamp and most popular of all collectables.

Collecting has moved forward and diversified by an enormous amount since those first postage stamps were issued and became sought after collectors items.

Nowadays almost every area of collecting has its own specialist group to cater for enthusiasts.

In this the first ever Guide to British Collecting Clubs we list full details of 108 specialist clubs, societies and associations that exist in Britain today.

These groups have memberships ranging from 7 to 70,000 and are almost exclusively organised by collectors for collectors. The majority publish regular newsletters, magazines and journals which contain a wealth of information, news and new contacts for collectors.

There is no doubt that if you are interested in learning more about, and increasing your collection then joining a club is one of the easiest and most enjoyable ways to do so.

Over 130 groups were initially contacted for inclusion in the guide. Some sadly no longer exist; others simply did not reply and a few declined to be entered. The remainder are listed with the details they supplied to our questionnaire, which are correct at the time of going to press.

We have tried to be as thorough as possible in our search for collecting clubs, but we may have missed some. If you are a member of a club that is not listed please send details for inclusion in our next edition.

LES HOOLE
Drighlington 1992

AMERICAN FOOTBALL PROGRAMME COLLECTORS CLUB

Address 26 Kettering Road, Burton Latimer, Northamptonshire NN15 5LP

Items Collected American Football Programmes and related memorabilia.

Year of Formation 1990.

Number of Members 84.

Annual Fees £7.00.

Meetings Held None.

Publications NEUTRAL ZONE is published in March, June, September and December with occasional updates. The A5 sized newsletter contains articles about American Football, details of new issues and members ads.

ANTIQUE COLLECTORS CLUB

Address	5 Church Street, Woodbridge, Suffolk IP12 1DS
Items Collected	Antiques.
Year of Formation	1966.
Number of Members	8,000.
Annual Fees	UK £17.50, Overseas £19.50, USA $35.00, Canada $45.00.
Meetings Held	None.
Publications	ANTIQUE COLLECTING is published 10 times a year. The magazine is extremely well produced with articles by the leading experts in the antique world.
	The Antique Collectors Club also publish a vast array of specialist books and guides on art and antiques. A catalogue of books is published annually.

ANTIQUE COLLECTING

The Journal of the Antique Collectors' Club

ASTRO SPACE STAMP SOCIETY

Address   32 Palleg Road, Lower Cwmtwrch, Swansea Valley, West Glamorgan SA9 2QE

Items Collected   Postage Stamps with the theme of Space Exploration, Astronomy and Rockets.

Year of Formation 1986.

Number of Members 250.

Annual Fees   £7.50 UK and Europe, £12.50 Overseas.
Junior Section (11 to 21) £6.50 and £11.50.

Meetings Held   None.

Publications   ORBIT newsletter is published quarterly. The magazine has details of new issues, members articles and adverts.

The society also publish the index of spacecraft on stamps, the index of astronomy and astronomers on stamps and a directory of space stamp collectors.

THE BADGE COLLECTORS CIRCLE

Address   3 Ellis Close, Bramblefields, Quorn, Loughborough, Leicestershire LE12

Items Collected   Non-Military Enamel and Button Badges.

Year of Formation 1980.

Number of Members

Annual Fees   £5.00.

Meetings Held   Swapmeets are held twice a year.

Publications   THE BADGER — the circles newsletter is published 6 times a year. The magazine contains details of new issues, articles and members adverts.

PLEASE MENTION HOOLE'S GUIDE
TO BRITISH COLLECTING CLUBS WHEN
WRITING TO A CLUB

INTERNATIONAL BANK NOTE SOCIETY

Address	43 Templars Crescent, London N3 3QR
Items Collected	Paper Money, Shares, Bonds and Cheques.
Year of Formation	1962.
Number of Members	4,000.
Annual Fees	£10.00, Junior (11 to 17) £5.00, Life Membership £165.00.
Meetings Held	Last Thursday of every month in the Victory Services Club, Marble Arch, London.
Publications	A newsletter is published bi-monthly and a journal quarterly.
	The society also publish occasional books and a membership directory.

NEW BAXTER SOCIETY

Address c/o Museum of Reading, Town Hall, Blagrave Street, Reading RG1 1QH

Items Collected Baxter and Licensee Prints and 19th Century Coloured Printing.

Year of Formation 1983.

Number of Members 125.

Annual Fees £8.00 Single, £12.00 Joint.

Meetings Held Meetings and visits are held twice a year.

Publications The society publish a well produced newsletter 3 times a year. The A4 sized magazine contains articles on the life and works of George Baxter, letters from members and adverts.

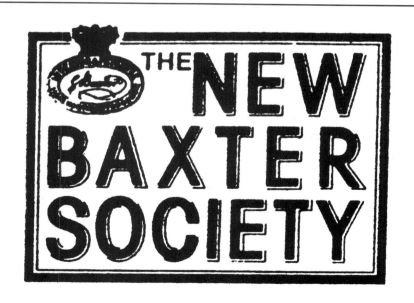

BRITISH BEER CAN COLLECTORS SOCIETY

Address	143 Linton Road, Loose, Maidstone, Kent ME15 0AS
Items Collected	Beer, Cider and Shandy Cans.
Year of Formation	1980.
Number of Members	68.
Annual Fees	£10.00.
Meetings Held	A monthly meeting is held at various venues around London. There is also an annual Cannection.
Publications	BEER CAN NEWS is published at various times. The magazine contains details of new issues and members ads.

THE OFFICIAL MAGAZINE OF THE
BRITISH BEER CAN COLLECTORS SOCIETY
BEER CAN News

NUMBER 7   JANUARY 1989

BRITISH BEER MAT COLLECTORS SOCIETY

Address   30 Carters Orchard, Quedeley,
                       Gloucester GL2 6WB

Items Collected   Beer Mats.

Year of Formation 1960.

Number of Members 400.

Annual Fees   £8.50.

Meetings Held   Meetings are held at almost 30 different venues on a
                       regular basis. There is also a National meeting
                       annually.

Publications   THE BEER MAT MAGAZINE is published monthly. The
                       magazine has details of all new issues, news of meetings
                       and members ads.

UNITED KINGDOM BELLEEK COLLECTORS GROUP

Address	5 Waterhall Avenue, Chingford, London E4 6NB
Items Collected	Irish Belleek, Parian China and Earthenware.
Year of Formation	1989.
Number of Members	100.
Annual Fees	£13.00 Worldwide Society plus £7.00 for UK affiliation.
Meetings Held	Meetings are held at members houses around the country 4 times a year.
Publications	The group publish a newsletter twice a year. New members receive a starter pack of back issues and minutes of meetings.

The Belleek Collectors' Society

UNITED KINGDOM COLLECTORS GROUP

BESWICK COLLECTORS CIRCLE

Address   Corner Cottage, Hedgerley Lane, Gerrards Cross, Buckinghamshire SL9 7NS

Items Collected   All Beswick Ware.

Year of Formation   1985.

Number of Members   500.

Annual Fees   £8.00 Single, £10.00 Double.

Meetings Held   Two main meetings are held in April and October. Various local get togethers are also arranged.

Publications   Two magazines are published annually in May and November. The newsletters contain articles and illustrations of Beswick Ware and news, sales and wants etc.

BICYCLE STAMPS CLUB

Address   162 Darley Avenue, Chorlton,
                            Manchester M21 2JH

Items Collected   Philatelic items featuring bicycles and bicycle related
                            subjects.

Year of Formation   1986.

Number of Members   Around 80 Worldwide, 25 in the UK.

Annual Fees   £11.00.

Meetings Held   None.

Publications   BICYCLE STAMPS is published quarterly. The A4 sized
                            newsletter has articles, new issues and recent
                            discoveries.

                            The club also publish check lists of all known cycle
                            related stamps.

Bicycle Stamps

ISSUE 10A - SPRING 1991

BIRD STAMP SOCIETY

Address	Lynmoor, Ampney Crucis, Cirencester, Gloucestershire GL7 5RY
Items Collected	Bird Stamps and related philatelic items.
Year of Formation	1986.
Number of Members	285.
Annual Fees	£14.00 UK, £18.00 Europe, £20.00 Overseas. Junior Membership (under 16) Half Price.
Meetings Held	Annual General Meeting held at Stampex meeting in London.
Publications	FLIGHT NEWSLETTER is issued quarterly. The 50/60 page newsletter contains articles, illustrations and adverts.
	BIRD THEME is also published quarterly and lists all new issues.

Vol.5 No.4 June 1991

THE BIRD STAMP SOCIETY.

FRIENDS OF BLUE

Address	10 Sea View Road, Herne Bay, Kent CT6 6JQ
Items Collected	Blue and White Transfer Printed Earthenware.
Year of Formation	1973.
Number of Members	350.
Annual Fees	£5.00 UK, £8.00 Overseas.
Meetings Held	One main meeting is held each year plus several smaller local meetings.
Publications	A bulletin is issued quarterly with articles and illustrations.
	Occasional papers relating to factories are produced.

PLEASE MENTION HOOLE'S GUIDE
TO BRITISH COLLECTING CLUBS WHEN
WRITING TO A CLUB

INTERNATIONAL BOND AND SHARE SOCIETY

Address   6/7 Castle Gates,
                         Shrewsbury SY1 2AE

Items Collected   Bonds and Share Certificates.

Year of Formation   1978.

Number of Members   500.

Annual Fees   £10.00 UK and Europe, £12.00 Overseas.

Meetings Held   First Tuesday of every month at the Ski Club, 118 Eaton Square, London SW1.

Publications   The society publish a journal bi-monthly.

REMEMBER
ALWAYS ENCLOSE A S.A.E. WHEN
WRITING TO A COLLECTING CLUB

THE BOOKPLATE SOCIETY

Address   11 Nella Road,
                     London W6 9PB

Items Collected Bookplates (ex-Libris).

Year of Formation 1891.

Number of Members 300.

Annual Fees   £25.00.

Meetings Held   Meetings are held 3 to 4 times a year with auctions held at 2 of them.

Publications   The society publish a newsletter quarterly and a journal twice a year. There is also an annual members book.

The journal contains articles, checklists, essays and reviews all of which are very well illustrated. The newsletter contains news of new issues, notes and queries, essays, details of exhibitions and members ads.

ASSOCIATION OF BOTTLED BEER COLLECTORS

Address	127 Victoria Park Road, Tunstall, Stoke on Trent ST6 6DY
Items Collected	Bottled Beer.
Year of Formation	1983.
Number of Members	150.
Annual Fees	£5.00.
Meetings Held	Five meetings a year are held at venues throughout the country.
Publications	WHAT'S BOTTLING is issued 6 times a year. The A5 sized magazine has details of new issues, articles, letters and members ads.

THE NEWSLETTER OF THE

What's Bottling

BUTTERFLY AND MOTH STAMP SOCIETY

Address	63 Dorchester Road, Garstang, Preston, Lancashire PR3 1HH
Items Collected	Stamps with Butterfly and/or Moth Motif.
Year of Formation	1985.
Number of Members	350.
Annual Fees	£6.00 in UK.
Meetings Held	None.
Publications	THE SWALLOWTAIL is published 3 times a year. The newsletter has articles, and details of new issues. The society also publish a country by country listing of all stamps with a Lepidopteran theme.
	The society, in conjunction with Stanley Gibbons, also produced the catalogue "Collect Butterflies and other insects on stamps".

Vol.4   THE SWALLOWTAIL   N°2

THE JOURNAL OF THE BUTTERFLY AND MOTH STAMP SOCIETY

ISSN 0952-7850   MAY 1992   WHOLE NUMBER 20

BRITISH BUTTON SOCIETY

Address	33 Haglane Copse, Pennington, Lymington SO41 8DR
Items Collected	Buttons and related themes.
Year of Formation	1976.
Number of Members	400.
Annual Fees	£10.00 UK, £15.00 Overseas Airmail, £12.00 Surface.
Meetings Held	AGM held last Saturday in March in London. Social meeting held first Saturday in October in London. Meetings are also held in Birmingham, Bristol, London and Hampshire at various times.
Publications	BUTTON LINES the societies journal is published 4 times a year. The A4 sized magazine has articles, letters, ads and many illustrations.
	The society also publish a membership directory and an index to the journal.

BUTTON LINES

The Journal of the
BRITISH   BUTTON   SOCIETY

The policy of this Journal is to promote free discussion on topics relative to the collection and preservation of buttons and research into their history. The Editor is not necessarily responsible for statements made in the Journal.

BYPOST COLLECTORS CLUB

Address   P.O. Box 1725,
Bristol BS17 5FA

Items Collected   Post Office memorabilia, models in pewter and diecast etc.

Year of Formation   1991.

Number of Members 600.

Annual Fees   £5.00.

Meetings Held   None.

Publications   A newsletter is published which has articles and details of all new issues.

BYGONE COLLECTORS MODELS

CANAL CARD COLLECTORS CIRCLE

Address   12 Wellstead Gardens, Westcliffe-on-Sea, Essex SS0 0AY

Items Collected Post Cards of Canals and their environs.

Year of Formation 1978.

Number of Members 50.

Annual Fees £4.00.

Meetings Held Annual Meeting held at a canal venue.

Publications GONGOOZLER is published quarterly. The A5 sized newsletter contains articles, details of cards and general news about the hobby.

CARTOPHILIC SOCIETY OF GREAT BRITAIN

Address 18 Hinstock Close, Farnborough, Hampshire GU14 0BE

Items Collected Cigarette and Trade Cards.

Year of Formation 1938.

Number of Members 1050.

Annual Fees £11.00.

Meetings Held Annual convention held last Saturday in April. There are also monthly meetings held by the 17 regional branches of the society.

Publications CARTOPHILIC NOTES AND NEWS is published bi-monthly. The magazine contains details of all the societies activities plus articles and adverts.

The society also publish a series of reference books detailing card issues since the 1880's.

BRITISH CHEQUE COLLECTORS SOCIETY

Address	71 Mile Lane, Coventry CV3 5GB
Items Collected	Cheques and Banking Ephemera.
Year of Formation	1981.
Number of Members	85.
Annual Fees	£8.00 Private, £15.00 Dealers.
Meetings Held	AGM in London during October. Regional meetings in the North and Midlands are also held.
Publications	COUNTERFOIL is an annual journal. There are also regular newsletters.

THE CIGARETTE PACKET COLLECTORS CLUB OF GREAT BRITAIN

Address	15 Dullington Road, Newmarket, Suffolk CB8 9JT
Items Collected	Cigarette Packets.
Year of Formation	1980.
Number of Members	220.
Annual Fees	£7.00.
Meetings Held	Regular meetings are held.
Publications	THE CIGARETTE PACKET the club newsletter is published bi-monthly. The well produced magazine has articles, new issues, members ads and club news.

ASSOCIATION OF COMIC ENTHUSIASTS

Address   c/o 17 Hill Street, Colne,
                     Lancashire BB8 0DH

Items Collected British Comics.

Year of Formation 1978.

Number of Members 280.

Annual Fees   £4.00.

Meetings Held   None.

Publications   COMIC CUTS the original journal of ACE has now merged with THE COMIC JOURNAL. The journal is published twice a year and contains a wealth of information about the comics of yesteryear. Each issue is very well illustrated.

Several guides to comic collecting are also published including full details of all comics and annuals issued by various publishers.

Incorporating

(The Association of Comic Enthusiasts)

THE COMMEMORATIVE COLLECTORS SOCIETY

Address 25 Farndale Close, Long Eaton, Nottingham NG10 3PA

Items Collected All forms of popular commemorabilia in Ceramic, Glass, Printed Fabric, Post Cards, Printed tin, enamel etc.

Year of Formation 1972.

Number of Members 3,672 in 32 different countries.

Annual Fees £12.00 Single, £15.00 Joint.

Meetings Held Meetings are held twice a year in spring and autumn at different venues.

Publications COLLECTING COMMEMORABILIA the societies journal is published quarterly. The large format magazine gives extensive news on new issues. There is also a newsletter published as and when necessary and special reviews for major events such as the 1977 silver jubilee of the Queen and Royal weddings.

PLEASE MENTION HOOLE'S GUIDE
TO BRITISH COLLECTING CLUBS WHEN
WRITING TO A CLUB

CORGI
COLLECTORS CLUB

Address   P.O. Box 323,
                       Swansea SA1 6BJ

Items Collected   Corgi Die-Cast Models.

Year of Formation 1984.

Number of Members 15,000.

Annual Fees   £12.50 UK, £14.50 Europe, £16.50 Rest of World

Meetings Held   Annual convention/swapmeet.

Publications   CORGI COLLECTOR the club's magazine is issued bi-
                       monthly. The well presented magazine has full details of
                       new issues, articles and members letters and ads.

THE
CRESTED CIRCLE

Address   42 Douglas Road, Tolworth, Surbiton,
                     Surrey KT6 7SA

Items Collected Crested China and commemoratives.

Year of Formation 1981.

Number of Members 500.

Annual Fees   £15.00.

Meetings Held   Four specialist fairs are held in March, May, September
                     and November at Twyford or Windsor.

Publications   THE CRESTED CIRCLE is a 40 page magazine that is
                     published 5 times a year. The A5 sized journal contains
                     news, views, postal auctions, a yellow pages section of
                     members ads.

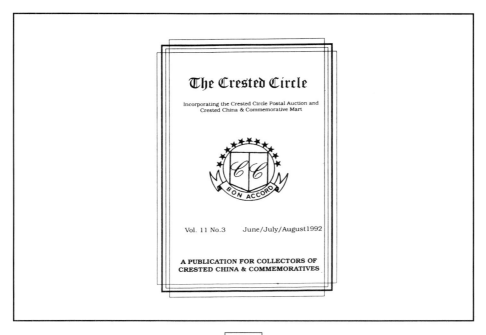

CRICKET MEMORABILIA
SOCIETY

Address   29 Highclere Road, Crumpsall,
                       Manchester M8 6WS

Items Collected   Cricket memorabilia.

Year of Formation 1987.

Number of Members 530.

Annual Fees   £10.00 UK, £15.00 Overseas.

Meetings Held   Four meetings a year are held between October and
                       April.

Publications   The society publish a magazine quarterly. The A5 sized
                       magazine has articles, news, letters and members ads.

THE INTERNATIONAL CROSBY CIRCLE

Address   19 Carrholm Crescent, Chapel Allerton,
                       Leeds LS7 2NL

Items Collected   All memorabilia connected with Bing Crosby.

Year of Formation 1950.

Number of Members 700.

Annual Fees   £7.00 UK, £8.00 Europe, $20.00 USA and Canada,
                       £11.50 Rest of World.

Meetings Held   Annual meeting and various local meetings.

Publications   BING is a glossy magazine published by the circle. The
                       circle have also published other books about Bing
                       Crosby.

REMEMBER
ALWAYS ENCLOSE A S.A.E. WHEN
WRITING TO A COLLECTING CLUB

CROWN IMPERIAL

Address   37 Wolsey Close, Southall,
                         Middlesex UB2 4NQ

Items Collected   Military Badges and Insignia.

Year of Formation   1973.

Number of Members   300.

Annual Fees   £9.00.

Meetings Held   Four meetings a year are held in London and York.

Publications   CROWN IMPERIAL JOURNAL is published quarterly.

EXCLUSIVE FIRST EDITIONS
OFFICIAL COLLECTORS CLUB

Address	Farmside, Witham Bank, Martindales, Woodhall Spa, Lincolnshire LN10 6XS
Items Collected	1/76th Scale Die-Cast Models produced by Exclusive First Editions.
Year of Formation	1991.
Number of Members	900.
Annual Fees	£13.00.
Meetings Held	None.
Publications	A newsletter is published monthly which gives details of new issues etc.
	There is also an annual collectors guide.

EFE

Exclusive **F**irst **E**ditions

Official Collectors Club

FIRE MARK
CIRCLE

Address c/o Royal Insurance, New Hall Place, Old Hall Street, Liverpool L69 3EN

Items Collected Fire Marks and Fire Fighting memorabilia.

Year of Formation 1934.

Number of Members 200.

Annual Fees £10.00 Joining Fee then £10.00 per annum.

Meetings Held AGM in London in April plus a meeting in October.

Publications A journal is published twice a year. The journal has news of the societies activities and letters from members etc.

JOURNAL/BULLETIN
OF THE FIRE MARK CIRCLE

Number 4   Autumn 1991

ASSOCIATION OF FOOTBALL BADGE COLLECTORS

Address	4 Renshaw Close, High Green, Sheffield, South Yorkshire S30 4FB
Items Collected	Enamel Football Lapel Badges.
Year of Formation	1980.
Number of Members	230.
Annual Fees	£8.00.
Meetings Held	AGM held in July and various other smaller meetings held throughout the year.
Publications	A newsletter is published monthly which gives details of all new issues.
	The association has also published a badge directory with photographs of over 3500 British Football Badges.

REMEMBER
ALWAYS ENCLOSE A S.A.E. WHEN
WRITING TO A COLLECTING CLUB

BRITISH SOCIETY OF FOOTBALL PHILATELY

Address	104 Sewerby Road, Bridlington YO16 5DA
Items Collected	Stamps and related philatelic items connected with football.
Year of Formation	1988.
Number of Members	40.
Annual Fees	£5.00 UK, £8.00 Overseas.
Meetings Held	Meetings are held on an irregular basis but the society meet at the annual thematica in London.
Publications	KICK OFF the societies newsletter is published 3 to 4 times a year. The magazine has details of new issues and articles etc.

FOOTBALL POSTCARD COLLECTORS CLUB

Address	173 Northumberland Avenue, North Harrow, Middlesex HA2 7RB
Items Collected	Football Postcards.
Year of Formation	1989.
Number of Members	100.
Annual Fees	£10.00.
Meetings Held	None.
Publications	The club issue a quarterly newsletter. The large format magazine contains articles, new issues, members letters and ads and many illustrations.
	The club have also published their own postcards.

ASSOCIATION OF FOOTBALL STATISTICIANS

Address	22 Bretons, Basildon, Essex SS15 5BY
Items Collected	Football Statistics and Memorabilia.
Year of Formation	1978.
Number of Members	1,200.
Annual Fees	£13.50 UK, £17.50 Overseas.
Meetings Held	Four meetings a year are held in London and several held at venues throughout the country.
Publications	A quarterly newsletter is published with news of the associations activities and letters, members ads etc.
	The association also publish a wide range of books and guides to football.

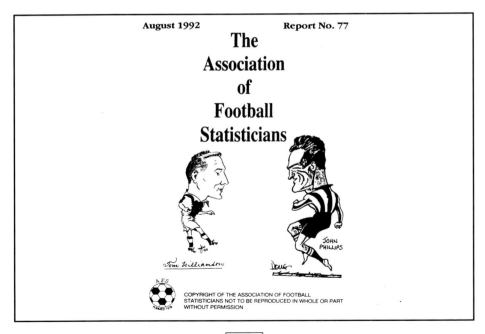

August 1992   Report No. 77

The Association of Football Statisticians

JOHN PHILLIPS

Tom Williamson

Doug

KING GEORGE VI COLLECTORS SOCIETY

Address   24 Stourwood Road, Southbourne, Bournemouth BH6 3QP

Items Collected   Stamps and Postal History of the King George VI era.

Year of Formation   1960.

Number of Members   300.

Annual Fees   £5.00 UK and Overseas Surface Mail, £8.00 Overseas Airmail.

Meetings Held   The society hold 3 meetings a year at the British Philatelic Centre, 107 Charterhouse Street, London and a further meeting in the North of England.

Publications   GEOSIX journal is published quarterly. The A5 sized journal has news of stamps, society news, letters, auction reports and ads.

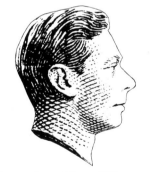

GEOSIX

NEWSLETTER
of
THE KING GEORGE VI COLLECTORS SOCIETY

INTERNATIONAL PHILATELIC GOLF SOCIETY

Address	'Caberfeidh', Riverside, Poolewe, Ross-shire IV22 2LA
Items Collected	Golf with philatelic connection.
Year of Formation	1986.
Number of Members	200.
Annual Fees	£6.00 UK, $10.00 USA commencing 1st July.
Meetings Held	Informal meetings are held at philatelic exhibitions when suitable.
Publications	TEE TIME journal is published. The A4 sized journal has details of new issues worldwide plus society news.

JOURNAL OF THE INTERNATIONAL PHILATELIC GOLF SOCIETY

GOSS COLLECTORS CLUB

Address	4 Khasiaberry, Walnut Tree, Milton Keynes, Buckinghamshire MK7 7DP
Items Collected	China made by W. H. Goss.
Year of Formation	1970.
Number of Members	810.
Annual Fees	£12.00.
Meetings Held	Two fairs are held in April and September and regional meetings are held intermittently.
Publications	GOSS HAWK magazine is published by the club.

GOSS AND CRESTED CHINA CLUB

Address   62 Murray Road, Horndean, Waterlooville,
                       Hampshire PO8 9JL

Items Collected   Antique Heraldic Souvenir Ware.

Year of Formation 1975.

Number of Members 1600.

Annual Fees   £12.00.

Meetings Held   Seasonal open days are held.

Publications   GOSS AND CRESTED CHINA is a monthly club
                       magazine with club news and details of items for sale.

                       The club also publish several guides to collecting
                       heraldic wares and also a book about the Staffordshire
                       potter William Henry Goss.

GRAND PRIX CONTACT CLUB

Address	26 Broom Road, Shirley, Croydon CR0 8NE
Items Collected	Motor Racing memorabilia, Books, Programmes, Models, Photographs etc.
Year of Formation	1985.
Number of Members	550.
Annual Fees	£12.50.
Meetings Held	The club hold several meetings and social functions at various locations.
Publications	GRAND PRIX WORLD the club magazine is published monthly. The magazine has details of club activities, race analysis, team and driver profiles and members ads.

HONITON POTTERY COLLECTORS SOCIETY

Address	112 Sylvan Avenue, London N22 5JB
Items Collected	Honiton and Dorset pottery.
Year of Formation	1985.
Number of Members	100.
Annual Fees	£8.00.
Meetings Held	The society hold 2 meetings a year.
Publications	A newsletter is published every 2 months.

HORNBY RAILWAY COLLECTORS ASSOCIATION

Address
2 Ravensmore Road, Sherwood, Nottingham NG5 2AH

Items Collected
Hornby "O" Gauge and Dublo Trains and Accessories produced by Meccano Ltd. 1920–1964.

Year of Formation
1969.

Number of Members
2,200

Annual Fees
£3.00 Joining Fee then £14.50.

Meetings Held
AGM in February and several local meetings at various locations.

Publications
THE HORNBY RAILWAY COLLECTOR is published 11 times a year, not January. The well produced magazine has details of club activities, letters, members ads etc. The association also publish THE DIRECTORY OF REPLACEMENT AND REPAIR SERVICES which is updated annually and free to members. The association also offer advisory services to members on all aspects of collecting Hornby.

NATIONAL HORSE BRASS SOCIETY

Address	12 Severndale, Droitwich Spa, Worcestershire WR9 8PD
Items Collected	Horse Brasses and Harness Decorations.
Year of Formation	1975.
Number of Members	550
Annual Fees	£12.00 Single, £16.00 Family UK. £18.00 Single, £22.00 Family Overseas.
Meetings Held	AGM held in March plus 3 to 4 regional meetings each year.
Publications	A journal is produced in June and December and a newsletter in March and September. The society has also published 7 books on Horse Brasses.

PLEASE MENTION HOOLE'S GUIDE
TO BRITISH COLLECTING CLUBS WHEN
WRITING TO A CLUB

UK HOT WHEELS COLLECTORS CLUB

Address   5a Belfray Avenue, Harefield, Middlesex UB9 6HY

Items Collected   "Hot Wheels" Cars and related items produced by Mattel Ltd.

Year of Formation   1989.

Number of Members   60

Annual Fees   £10.00 UK, £7.50 under 16 UK, £17.50 Overseas.

Meetings Held   AGM and swapmeets.

Publications   A magazine is issued quarterly with news of new issues and older models.

HOVERMAIL COLLECTORS CLUB

Address	20 Crabtree Lodge, Crabtree Lane, Lancing, Sussex BN15 9NG
Items Collected	Mail, ie Philatelic Covers carried by Hovercraft.
Year of Formation	1970.
Number of Members	25
Annual Fees	£5.00.
Meetings Held	AGM in September.
Publications	SLIPSTREAM is published quarterly.

REMEMBER
ALWAYS ENCLOSE A S.A.E. WHEN
WRITING TO A COLLECTING CLUB

INDIAN MILITARY COLLECTORS SOCIETY

Address   37 Wolsey Close, Southall,
                     Middlesex UB2 4NQ

Items Collected Military Insignia from the Indian Sub-Continent.

Year of Formation 1983.

Number of Members 100

Annual Fees   £8.00.

Meetings Held   Two meetings a year are held, at the National Army Museum, London.

Publications   DURBAR the society's newsletter is published quarterly.

BENEVOLENT CONFRATERNITY OF DISSECTOLOGISTS

Address   32 The Limes, Rushmere St. Andrews, Ipswich,
                     Suffolk IP5 7EA

Items Collected Jigsaw Puzzles.

Year of Formation 1985.

Number of Members 165

Annual Fees   £2.00 Joining Fee then £1.00.

Meetings Held   Meetings and swapmeets are held quarterly.

Publications   Three newsletters a year are published and one annual magazine.

JUDGES POSTCARD STUDY GROUP

Address   8 Parkhill Road, Ewell,
                       Epsom KT17 1LG

Items Collected   Judges Postcards and related themes.

Year of Formation 1981.

Number of Members 30

Annual Fees   £4.00.

Meetings Held   AGM held in Summer in South East England.

Publications   A newsletter is published 3 times a year. The A4 sized newsletter has information on new cards that members have discovered and club news, letters etc.

                       The club also produce a list of Judges Postcards by number and title.

Judges' Postcards STUDY GROUP

THE LABOLOGISTS SOCIETY

Address   20 Tongdean Road, Hove,
East Sussex BN3 6QE

Items Collected   Labels, especially Beer Bottle Labels.

Year of Formation   1958.

Number of Members 300

Annual Fees   £6.00, Under 16 and Over 65 £3.00.

Meetings Held   Four meetings a year are held usually in London. An annual Label of the Year meeting is also held in October. There are several local meetings.

Publications   A newsletter is published 6 times a year. The A5 sized magazine has details of new issues, articles, members ads, letters and special offers.

The society also publish lists of British and overseas breweries.

THE LACE GUILD

Address	The Hollies, 53 Audnam, Stourbridge, West Midlands DY8 4AE
Items Collected	Lace and Lace related items.
Year of Formation	1976.
Number of Members	9,000 Adults, 425 Juniors
Annual Fees	£14.00 UK, £18.00 Europe, £22.00 Overseas. Junior (under 18) £4.00 UK, £7.00 Europe, £8.00 Overseas.
Meetings Held	AGM held in April.
Publications	LACE the guilds magazine is published quarterly. The well produced magazine has details of club news and events and numerous articles and ads. The guild occasionally publish instruction books.

LETTER BOX STUDY GROUP

Address	43 Miall Road, Hall Green, Birmingham, West Midlands B28 9BS
Items Collected	Postboxes, full size and miniatures and other items connected with the Royal Mail.
Year of Formation	1976.
Number of Members	700.
Annual Fees	£3.50 Single, £4.00 Family.
Meetings Held	Two meetings a year are held.
Publications	The group publish a quarterly newsletter. The A4 sized magazine gives details of the groups activities and letters and articles from members.

The Letter Box Study Group

INTERNATIONAL MAP COLLECTORS SOCIETY

Address	43 Templars Crescent, London N3 3QR
Items Collected	Old Maps, Globes and Atlases.
Year of Formation	1981.
Number of Members	1,000.
Annual Fees	£4.00 Joining Fee then £16.00, Junior (under 21) £8.00.
Meetings Held	Annual meeting held in London. Occasional meetings held throughout the country.
Publications	The society publish a quarterly magazine. A catalogue for the annual meeting is also published.

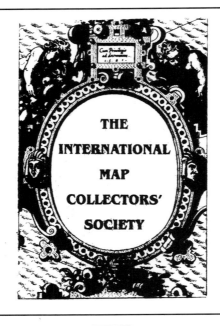

GREAT BRITAIN MAP POSTCARD CLUB

Address	12 Rose Grove, Beeston Rylands, Nottingham NG9 1UB
Items Collected	Postcards with a map content.
Year of Formation	1990.
Number of Members	7.
Annual Fees	£10.00.
Meetings Held	AGM is held at the modern postcard fair in Nottingham.
Publications	THE EXPLORER newsletter is published monthly. The members of the club all play a very active part in compiling lists of cards available in their area. All new members are expected to do the same.

MATCHBOX INTERNATIONAL COLLECTORS ASSOCIATION

Address 13a Lower Bridge Street,
Chester CH1 1RS.

Items Collected Matchbox Toys and Models.

Year of Formation 1985.

Number of Members 8,000.

Annual Fees £14.00.

Meetings Held An annual convention is held. There is also similar conventions held in Germany, USA and Australia.

Publications Six colour magazines a year are issued. The association also publish books and price guides to the hobby.

PLEASE MENTION HOOLE'S GUIDE
TO BRITISH COLLECTING CLUBS WHEN
WRITING TO A CLUB

THE BRITISH MATCHBOX LABEL AND BOOKLET SOCIETY

Address	122 High Street, Melbourn, Royston, Hertfordshire SG8 6AL
Items Collected	Matchbox Labels, Match Booklets, hardware and ephemera connected with matches.
Year of Formation	1945.
Number of Members	700.
Annual Fees	Adults £6.50, Senior Citizens £3.50, Under 16 £3.00.
Meetings Held	Four meetings a year are held at the Victory Services Club in London. Local meetings are held at regular intervals.
Publications	The society publish a monthly newsletter. The society also publish a very large range of books and booklets associated with the hobby.

NEWSLETTER

OF THE

BRITISH MATCHBOX LABEL & BOOKLET SOCIETY

FOUNDED 1945

Vol. XXXV   Price £ 1.00   No. 273   JUNE, 1992

MAUCHLINE WARE COLLECTORS CLUB

Address   Unit 37, Romsey Industrial Estate, Greatbridge Road, Romsey, Hampshire SO51 0HR

Items Collected   Scottish Souvenir Woodware.

Year of Formation   1985.

Number of Members   200.

Annual Fees   £8.50.

Meetings Held   Weekend 'get togethers' are held at 18 month intervals.

Publications   The club publish 3 newsletters a year with details of club activities, articles, details of fairs and adverts.

MILITARY HERALDRY SOCIETY

Address	37 Wolsey Close, Southall, Middlesex UB2 4NQ
Items Collected	Cloth Formation Signs and similar cloth insignia.
Year of Formation	1951.
Number of Members	300.
Annual Fees	£6.00 Joining Fee then £4.00.
Meetings Held	Four meetings a year are held at the Polish Institute, London.
Publications	FORMATION SIGN is published quarterly.

UNITED KINGDOM MINI BOTTLE CLUB

Address	47 Burradon Road, Burradon, Cramlington, Northumberland NE23 7NF
Items Collected	Miniature Bottles, Figurals and Ceramics.
Year of Formation	1980.
Number of Members	460.
Annual Fees	£12.00 UK, £15.00 Europe, £18.00 USA and Canada, £19.00 Australia and New Zealand.
Meetings Held	AGM held over 3 days in Blackpool each May. Several local meetings held in England and Scotland.
Publications	A regular newsletter is produced.

MUG COLLECTORS ASSOCIATION

Address	Whitecroft, Chandler Road, Stoke Holy Cross, Norwich NR14 8RG
Items Collected	Advertising Mugs and other promotional ceramics.
Year of Formation	1982.
Number of Members	100.
Annual Fees	None.
Meetings Held	None.
Publications	No formal newsletter is produced but the club do have a list of collectors. The club functions through correspondence between all the members.

REMEMBER
ALWAYS ENCLOSE A S.A.E. WHEN
WRITING TO A COLLECTING CLUB

PHILATELIC MUSIC CIRCLE

Address	11 Aberdeen Grove, Armley, Leeds LS12 3QY
Items Collected	Music Philately.
Year of Formation	1969.
Number of Members	500.
Annual Fees	£7.50.
Meetings Held	AGM and convention held in London plus 2 regional meetings each year.
Publications	THE BATON the circles magazine is published 3 times a year. Each issue has details of new issues, articles, illustrations and members ads.

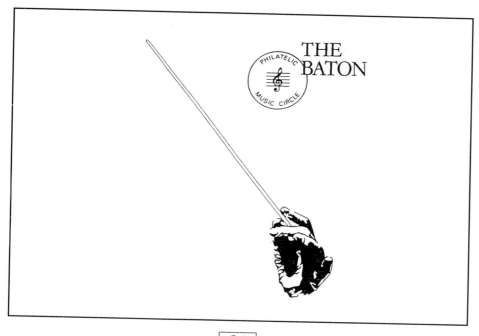

MUSICAL BOX SOCIETY OF GREAT BRITAIN

Address	P.O. Box 299, Waterbeach, Cambridge CB4 4PJ
Items Collected	Musical Boxes, Barrel Organs, Pianolas and all mechanical musical instruments.
Year of Formation	1962.
Number of Members	800.
Annual Fees	£10.00 Joining Fee then £25.00.
Meetings Held	Four meetings a year are held.
Publications	THE MUSIC BOX magazine is published quarterly. The well produced magazine contains articles, illustrations, society news, letters and adverts.

THE MUZZLE LOADERS ASSOCIATION OF GREAT BRITAIN

Address   P.O. Box 493, Rhyl,
                     Clwyd LL18 5XG

Items Collected Firearms, their accessories, literature etc that pre-dates 1870.

Year of Formation 1952.

Number of Members 1,800.

Annual Fees   £3.00 Joining Fee then £15.00.

Meetings Held   Branch meetings are held throughout the country.

Publications   BLACK POWDER the annual journal is a very well produced magazine giving details of collections, association news and details of branch meetings. The society also publish an equally well produced newsletter 6 times a year.

The Official Journal of
The Muzzle Loaders' Association of Great Britain

A perfect gift to start the hobby of a lifetime

Coin collecting is one of the most absorbing and rewarding of pursuits but whether you are an established collector or wish to introduce a friend to a hobby for life, the Royal Mint Starter Pack will be of interest to you.

Affordably priced at just £25.95, the pack contains a set of Brilliant Uncirculated coins from overseas, the 1992 coin set for the United Kingdom and two informative publications suitable for new and seasoned collectors alike.

To order or to send for your FREE illustrated brochure, see coupon below. *(N.B. – Items may vary from those illustrated).*

ROYAL NUMISMATIC SOCIETY

Address   c/o Department of Coins, Medals,
                       The British Museum, London WC1B 3DG

Items Collected   Coins.

Year of Formation 1836.

Number of Members 1,000.

Annual Fees   £18.00.

Meetings Held   Monthly meetings are held.

Publications   NUMISMATIC CHRONICLE is published annually.

PLEASE MENTION HOOLE'S GUIDE
TO BRITISH COLLECTING CLUBS WHEN
WRITING TO A CLUB

OLD BILL NEWSLETTER

Address Onslows, Metrostore, Townmead Road, London SW6 2RZ

Items Collected All drawings, china, postcards, printed ephemera, and other material relating to Old Bill and Bruce Bairnsfather.

Year of Formation 1987.

Number of Members 70.

Annual Fees £7.50.

Meetings Held Small informal gatherings are occasionally held in London.

Publications OLD BILL newsletter is published bi-monthly. The newsletter contains articles on the life and works of Bruce Bairnsfather, news of finds, checklists and members ads.

Vol. 4 no 6 November–December 1990

SOCIETY OF OLYMPIC COLLECTORS

Address	258 Torrisholme Road, Lancaster LA1 2TU
Items Collected	Olympic Philately, Memorabilia and Postcards.
Year of Formation	1984.
Number of Members	270.
Annual Fees	UK £5.00, Europe £6.00, Rest of World £9.00.
Meetings Held	AGM at Thematica in London.
Publications	TORCHBEARER is published quarterly. The society also publish supplements to Torch Bearer and hold quarterly postal auctions.

REMEMBER
ALWAYS ENCLOSE A S.A.E. WHEN
WRITING TO A COLLECTING CLUB

OPHTHALMIC ANTIQUES
INTERNATIONAL COLLECTORS CLUB

Address   3 Moor Park Road, Northwood,
                       Middlesex HA6 2DL

Items Collected   Antiques related to optics and vision.

Year of Formation 1982.

Number of Members 125.

Annual Fees   £6.00 UK, £10.00 Overseas.

Meetings Held   None.

Publications   A newsletter is published quarterly. The club also
                       publish 'COLLECTING OPHTHALMIC ANTIQUES' a
                       56 page guide for beginners.

OPHTHALMIC ANTIQUES
INTERNATIONAL
COLLECTORS CLUB
NEWSLETTER

THE ORDERS AND MEDALS RESEARCH SOCIETY

Address   123 Turnpike Link,
                         Croydon CR0 5NU

Items Collected   British and Foreign Orders, Decorations and Medals.

Year of Formation   1942.

Number of Members   2,800.

Annual Fees   £12.00 UK, £14.00 Overseas Surface Mail.
                         $20.00 Overseas Mail.

Meetings Held   Monthly meeting held at National Army museum.

Publications   The society publish a well produced quarterly journal with articles, news and ads.

                         The society also publish the miscellany of honours and an occasional membership list and handbook.

PLEASE MENTION HOOLE'S GUIDE
TO BRITISH COLLECTING CLUBS WHEN
WRITING TO A CLUB

69

CAMBRIDGE PAPERWEIGHT CIRCLE

Address	34 Huxley Road, Welling, Kent DA16 2EW
Items Collected	Antique and Modern Glass Paperweights.
Year of Formation	1981.
Number of Members	120.
Annual Fees	£5.00.
Meetings Held	Four meetings a year are held 2 in Spring and 2 in Autumn. The circle also arrange visits to artists and manufacturers and hold an exhibition every 3 years.
Publications	A newsletter is published quarterly. The circle also publish a catalogue for the exhibition held.

REMEMBER
ALWAYS ENCLOSE A S.A.E. WHEN
WRITING TO A COLLECTING CLUB

PASSENGER SHIP ENTHUSIAST ASSOCIATION

Address P.O. Box 358, Coulsdon, Surrey CR5 1AW

Items Collected Shipping memorabilia.

Year of Formation 1987.

Number of Members 400.

Annual Fees £12.00.

Meetings Held Monthly meeting held onboard *Kathleen May,* Southwark Quay, London. AGM at annual ship show, Westminster Central Hall, London.

Publications SEA LINES the associations magazine is published quarterly. The association also produce video films of current and yesterdays liners.

Several cruises, weekend ferry trips and lunches are also arranged.

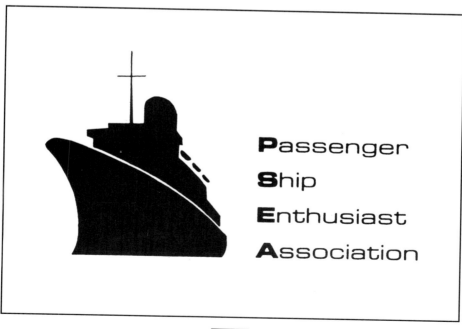

Passenger
Ship
Enthusiast
Association

GREAT BRITAIN PHILATELIC SOCIETY

Address	6b Oatlands Chase, Weybridge, Surrey KT13 9SA
Items Collected	Stamps and Postal History of Great Britain.
Year of Formation	1956.
Number of Members	750.
Annual Fees	£20.00 UK, £21.00 Europe, £26.00 Rest of World.
Meetings Held	Monthly meeting held in London plus several regional meetings.
Publications	The society publish a journal and newsletter 6 times a year. There are also several books and guides produced.

PLEASE MENTION HOOLE'S GUIDE
TO BRITISH COLLECTING CLUBS WHEN
WRITING TO A CLUB

NATIONAL PHILATELIC SOCIETY

Address	107 Charterhouse Street, London EC1M 6PT
Items Collected	British, British Colonial and Foreign Stamps.
Year of Formation	1899.
Number of Members	1,050.
Annual Fees	£19.50.
Meetings Held	Monthly meeting held with the exception of August at the society's headquarters.
Publications	STAMP LOVER is published 6 times a year. The society also hold monthly auctions and have one of the finest libraries on philatelic matters in the UK.

BRITISH TELECOM PHONECARD COLLECTORS CLUB

Address	Camelford House, 87 Albert Embankment, London SE1 7TS
Items Collected	BT Phonecards.
Year of Formation	1989.
Number of Members	4,000.
Annual Fees	None — Membership is free.
Meetings Held	None.
Publications	A well produced newsletter is published every 2 months. The newsletter contains details of all new issues, special offers, check lists and members ads.

THE PHOTOGRAPHIC COLLECTORS CLUB OF GREAT BRITAIN

Address 5 Station Industrial Estate, Low Prudhoe, Northumberland NE42 6NP

Items Collected Photographic equipment and images.

Year of Formation 1977.

Number of Members 1,000.

Annual Fees £18.00.

Meetings Held National and local meetings are held.

Publications The club publish PHOTOGRAPHICA WORLD a well produced quarterly magazine and a newsletter TAILBOARD.

THE ENGLISH PLAYING CARD SOCIETY

Address	11 Pierrepont Street, Bath, Avon BA1 1LA
Items Collected	English Playing Cards, Card Games and Ephemera.
Year of Formation	1984.
Number of Members	165.
Annual Fees	£18.00 UK, £20.00 Europe, £25.00 Rest of World.
Meetings Held	Two meetings a year are held in Bath.
Publications	A newsletter is produced quarterly. The newsletter has details of new issues, articles on older issues and ads.

REMEMBER
ALWAYS ENCLOSE A S.A.E. WHEN
WRITING TO A COLLECTING CLUB

INTERNATIONAL PLAYING CARD SOCIETY

Address	43 Templars Crescent, London N3 3QR
Items Collected	Playing Cards, Tarot Cards, Games and Books.
Year of Formation	1972.
Number of Members	1,000.
Annual Fees	£17.00 UK, £20.00 Rest of World.
Meetings Held	Quarterly meetings are held in London and Edinburgh. AGM held in London.
Publications	The society publish a quarterly newsletter and journal. Both publications are well produced and illustrated and contain many articles, news and ads.
	The society also publish occasional monographs.

POLAR SYSTEM HISTORY SOCIETY OF GREAT BRITAIN

Address　　　　　　46 New Village Road, Cottingham,
　　　　　　　　　　　East Yorkshire HU16 4NA

Items Collected　　 Stamps of postal history of the polar regions.

Year of Formation　1952.

Number of Members　400.

Annual Fees　　　　£3.00 UK, £5.00 Overseas Surface Mail, £13.00 Airmail.

Meetings Held　　　Two meetings a year are held in London.

Publications　　　　POLAR POST the society's newsletter is published quarterly. The magazine contains details of new issues, articles and offers of stamps and special covers.

Published quarterly by the
**POLAR POSTAL
HISTORY SOCIETY OF
GREAT BRITAIN**

VOLUME 24 NUMBER 2

WHOLE NUMBER 153

JUNE 1992

POLICE INSIGNIA COLLECTORS ASSOCIATION OF GREAT BRITAIN

Address   43 Hunters Way, Saffron Walden,
                         Essex CB11 4DE

Items Collected   Police Badges, Uniforms and Insignia.

Year of Formation   1974.

Number of Members   470.

Annual Fees   £8.00 UK, £10.00 Europe, £12.00 Rest of World plus
                         Initial Joining Fee of £5.00.

Meetings Held   None.

Publications   PICA magazine is published 3 times a year.

PLEASE MENTION HOOLE'S GUIDE
TO BRITISH COLLECTING CLUBS WHEN
WRITING TO A CLUB

GREAT BRITAIN POSTCARD CLUB

Address	34 Harper House, St. James Crescent, London SW9 7LW
Items Collected	Postcards.
Year of Formation	1961.
Number of Members	500.
Annual Fees	£7.00.
Meetings Held	None.
Publications	POSTCARD WORLD the club magazine is published 6 times a year. The magazine has members ads, details of new issues and discoveries and well illustrated articles.

POSTCARD WORLD

Journal of The Postcard Club of Gt Britain

BRITISH POSTMARK SOCIETY

Address	21 Empress Way, Euxton, Chorley, Lancashire PR7 6QB
Items Collected	British Postmarks.
Year of Formation	1958.
Number of Members	343.
Annual Fees	50p Joining Fee then £6.00.
Meetings Held	Four meetings a year are held at The Victory Service Club in London.
Publications	The society publish a quarterly Bulletin which gives full details of new postmarks, special issues and many illustrations. Included with the Bulletin is a Society News supplement which has members ads as well as society news.
	The society have also published several books and guides to postmark collecting.

POSTAL ORDER SOCIETY

Address
15 Witch Close, East Stour, Gillingham, Dorset SP8 5LB

Items Collected
Postal Orders, Money Orders and Reply Coupons.

Year of Formation
1984.

Number of Members
50.

Annual Fees
£5.00.

Meetings Held
The AGM is held at the Great Western Royal Hotel in London in October.

Publications
POSTAL ORDER NEWS the societies newsletter is published quarterly. The 20 page issue contains many illustrated articles about Postal Orders etc. worldwide.

REMEMBER
ALWAYS ENCLOSE A S.A.E. WHEN
WRITING TO A COLLECTING CLUB

RAFLET STAMP CLUB

Address	Swiss Cottage, Sutton Road, Huttoft, Alford, Lincolnshire LN13 9RG
Items Collected	Stamps, Covers, Postcards and Ephemera.
Year of Formation	1958.
Number of Members	1,100.
Annual Fees	£5.00 Senior, £2.50 Junior (under 18).
Meetings Held	None.
Publications	The club publish a bulletin 10 times a year. The well produced magazine contains articles on new issues from around the world, letters and members ads.

Founded by the late
A.G.GROOM
Hon Sec.1958-1988

AUGUST 1992

BULLETIN

RAILWAY PHILATELIC GROUP

Address	12 Mapelwell Drive, Leicester LE4 1BD
Items Collected	Philatelic material relating to railways.
Year of Formation	1966.
Number of Members	450.
Annual Fees	£6.50.
Meetings Held	AGM and exhibition.
Publications	RAILWAY PHILATELY magazine is published quarterly. The magazine has full details of new issues, articles and members and dealers adverts. The society also publish several books and guides.

RAILWAY
PHILATELY

ISSN 0951-886X

The Journal of the Railway Philatelic Group

ROYAL DOULTON INTERNATIONAL COLLECTORS SOCIETY

Address   Minton House, London Road, Stoke on Trent, Staffordshire ST4 7QD

Items Collected   All Royal Doulton products, especially figures and character jugs.

Year of Formation   1980.

Number of Members

Annual Fees   £15.00 for first year then £12.50.

Meetings Held   None.

Publications   GALLERY the clubs magazine is published quarterly. The full colour large format magazine contains articles, news, members letters and details of new issues. There is also a quarterly newsletter which contains details of collectors fairs etc. and a members adverts section.

                               The club commissions four special pieces per year from Royal Doulton which are exclusive to members.

BRITISH ROYAL PORTRAITS STUDY GROUP

Address 62a Bridge Street, Pershore, Worcestershire WR10 1AX

Items Collected Stamps, Post Cards, Postal Stationery.

Year of Formation 1977.

Number of Members 36.

Annual Fees £4.00 UK, £6.00 Europe, $12.00 USA.

Meetings Held None.

Publications Five newsletters a year are published containing details of new issues etc.

The group have also published THE ROYAL IMAGE, stamp portraits of British Monarchs from Edward the Confessor to Elizabeth the Second.

PLEASE MENTION HOOLE'S GUIDE
TO BRITISH COLLECTING CLUBS WHEN
WRITING TO A CLUB

RUGBY LEAGUE COLLECTORS FEDERATION

Address	6 The Stray, Idle, Bradford, West Yorkshire
Items Collected	All Rugby League memorabilia.
Year of Formation	1978.
Number of Members	350.
Annual Fees	£5.00.
Meetings Held	Collectors fairs are held at various venues from September to May.
Publications	A newsletter is published bi-monthly with articles, details of programmes issued, members letters and adverts. The federation also publish a very detailed and well produced members register.

GUILD OF
ST. GABRIEL

Address   230 Powder Mill Lane, Twickenham, Middlesex TW2 6EJ

Items Collected   Postal material of religious interest.

Year of Formation   1954.

Number of Members   125.

Annual Fees   £10.00.

Meetings Held   Monthly meetings are held in London and Birmingham.

Publications   The guild publish a quarterly bulletin which contains news and views, and several illustrations of new issues.

The guild also publish 'Faith Art Philately' a guide to collecting religion on stamps. There are also check lists for Easter and Christmas stamp issues.

GABRIEL

RELIGION ON STAMPS

1992

THE
SHELLY GROUP

Address   228 Croyland Road, Lower Edmonton,
London N9 7BG

Items Collected   Wares of the Shelly Potteries.

Year of Formation   1986.

Number of Members

Annual Fees   £10.00.

Meetings Held   None.

Publications   A quarterly newsletter is published.

REMEMBER
ALWAYS ENCLOSE A S.A.E. WHEN
WRITING TO A COLLECTING CLUB

SHIP STAMP
SOCIETY

Address 33a Ridgeway Road, Timperley, Altrincham, Cheshire WA15 7HA

Items Collected Ships on stamps and all associated material.

Year of Formation 1970.

Number of Members 225.

Annual Fees £10.00 UK, £9.00 Overseas Surface Mail.

Meetings Held AGM held in May and a monthly meeting held in Merseyside.

Publications THE LOG BOOK magazine is published monthly. The magazine has details of new issues, articles and adverts.

THE
L⊜G BOOK

OFFICIAL MAGAZINE OF THE SHIP STAMP SOCIETY

MEMBER OF B.T.A. and I.F.M.P.

THE SILHOUETTE COLLECTORS CLUB

Address   Flat 5, 13 Brunswick Square, Hove,
                     East Sussex BN3 1EH

Items Collected English Silhouettes of every kind and period.

Year of Formation 1967.

Number of Members 40.

Annual Fees   £5.00.

Meetings Held   Three meetings a year are held which usually take the
                     form of a visit to a collection.

Publications   A newsletter is published 3 times a year which gives
                     details of club news and views, auction news and
                     articles.

PLEASE MENTION HOOLE'S GUIDE
TO BRITISH COLLECTING CLUBS WHEN
WRITING TO A CLUB

THE SILVER SPOON CLUB OF GREAT BRITAIN

Address   Glenleigh Park, Sticker, St. Austell,
Cornwall PL26 7JB

Items Collected   Antique and other fine silver spoons.

Year of Formation   1989.

Number of Members   125.

Annual Fees   £29.50 UK, £35.50 Europe, £37.50 North America,
£39.50 Australia.

Meetings Held   None.

Publications   THE FINIAL is a monthly newsletter with articles, news
and views and sales reviews.

The Silver Spoon Club
(OF GREAT BRITAIN)

THE
SPODE SOCIETY

Address
P.O. Box 1812,
London NW4 4NP

Items Collected
Spode, Copeland Pottery and Porcelain.

Year of Formation
1986.

Number of Members
200.

Annual Fees
£12.00 Single, £17.00 Joint at one address.

Meetings Held
AGM in May plus several other events.

Publications
The society publish two magazines THE SPODE SOCIETY RECORDER and THE SPODE SOCIETY REVIEW. The society have a series of events throughout the year including talks, weekends and lectures.

The Spode Society

UNITED KINGDOM SPOON COLLECTORS CLUB

Address	15 West Street, Pontypridd, Mid Glamorgan CF37 4PS
Items Collected	Spoons.
Year of Formation	1980.
Number of Members	500.
Annual Fees	£8.00 Ordinary, £6.00 OAP, £11.00 Overseas.
Meetings Held	AGM in October, half yearly in May plus several local meetings.
Publications	A magazine is published every 2 months.

REMEMBER
ALWAYS ENCLOSE A S.A.E. WHEN
WRITING TO A COLLECTING CLUB

STAMP BUG CLUB

Address FREEPOST,
Northampton NN3 1BR

Items Collected Stamps.

Year of Formation 1980.

Number of Members 70,000.

Annual Fees For Children aged 7 to 14 only.
£3.50 for 2 years, £5.00 for 5 years in UK, £8.50 for 2 years, £12.50 for 5 years Overseas.
Group Membership (10 plus) £2.20 each for 2 years, £3.50 each for 5 years.

Meetings Held None.

Publications STAMP BUG NEWS the clubs magazine is published bi-monthly. The well produced full colour magazine has details of new issues, club news, competitions, quizzes and occasional free gifts.

SYLVAC
COLLECTORS CIRCLE

Address   174 Portsmouth Road, Horndean,
                       Hampshire PO8 9HP

Items Collected   Sylvac ware and early Shaw and Copestake items.

Year of Formation 1988.

Number of Members 300.

Annual Fees   £8.00 UK, £12 Overseas.

Meetings Held   None.

Publications   The circle publish a quarterly newsletter with illustrated
                       articles about the hobby and members adverts.

                       The circle have also published an introduction to
                       Sylvac.

BRITISH TEDDY BEAR ASSOCIATION

Address	P.O. Box 290, Brighton BN2 1DR
Items Collected	Teddy Bears.
Year of Formation	1991.
Number of Members	2,000.
Annual Fees	£12.00.
Meetings Held	None.
Publications	BEARINGS the associations magazine is published quarterly. The magazine has articles, new issues, and members adverts. Membership includes the UK Teddy Bear guide and a bear making manual.

THE THIMBLE GUILD

Address	Thistle Mill, Biggar, Lanarkshire ML12 6LP
Items Collected	Thimbles.
Year of Formation	1983.
Number of Members	20,000.
Annual Fees	None.
Meetings Held	None.
Publications	A commercial club that issues a customers brochure for new thimbles issued. The club also publish a newsletter with letters from members.

PLEASE MENTION HOOLE'S GUIDE
TO BRITISH COLLECTING CLUBS WHEN
WRITING TO A CLUB

THIMBLE SOCIETY
OF LONDON

Address   Unit 34, Grays Antique Market, 58 Davies Street, London W1Y 1LB

Items Collected Thimbles and Sewing Tools (not sewing machines).

Year of Formation 1981.

Number of Members 1,000.

Annual Fees   £16.00 UK, £18.00 Europe, £20.00 Rest of World.

Meetings Held   AGM weekend in London.

Publications   The society publish a quarterly magazine. The well produced magazine has articles and many photographs of thimbles.

REMEMBER
ALWAYS ENCLOSE A S.A.E. WHEN
WRITING TO A COLLECTING CLUB

INTERNATIONAL COLLECTORS OF TIME ASSOCIATION

Address   173 Coleheme Court, Redcliffe Gardens,
                       London SW5 0DX

Items Collected   Wristwatches, Cigarette Lighters and Costume
                       Jewellery.

Year of Formation 1990.

Number of Members 3,400.

Annual Fees   US $100.00.

Meetings Held   Meetings are held in England, USA and Hong Kong.

Publications   TIME TALK the associations bi-monthly magazine is a
                       very well produced glossy publication.

                       Several collectors reference books are available through
                       the association.

BRITISH TITANIC
SOCIETY

Address   P.O. Box 401, Hope Carr Way, Leigh,
Lancashire WN7 5WW

Items Collected Anything connected with the steamship Titanic and her
sister ships.

Year of Formation 1986.

Number of Members 500.

Annual Fees   £10.00 UK, £15.00 Overseas.

Meetings Held Annual convention in Southampton.

Publications   ATLANTIC DAILY BULLETIN is published quarterly.
The journal contains news of the society's activities and
articles etc.

TORQUAY POTTERY COLLECTORS SOCIETY

Address

Torre Abbey, Torquay, Devon

Items Collected

Pottery made in South Devon c1870–1960.

Year of Formation

1976.

Number of Members

1,400.

Annual Fees

£8.00 Single, £10.00 Double.

Meetings Held

Three national and 3 to 4 regional meetings are held each year. There is also a bi-annual symposium in the UK.

Publications

The society publish a quarterly magazine with articles, illustrations, news and views and adverts.

The society have also published several guides to collecting Torquay pottery.

TRAIN COLLECTORS SOCIETY

Address   29 Lammas Way, Ampthill,
                       Bedfordshire MK45 2TR

Items Collected   Model Trains: any make, any gauge, any age.

Year of Formation 1979.

Number of Members 160.

Annual Fees   £8.00.

Meetings Held   Two main meetings are held each year.

Publications   TCS NEWS the society's newsletter is published 6 times
                       a year. The magazine contains articles, news of society
                       activities and adverts.

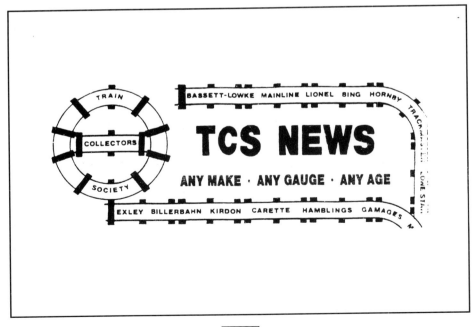

THE TRANSPORT TICKET SOCIETY

Address

4 Gladridge Close, Earley,
Reading RG6 2DL

Items Collected

Tickets from all modes of transport, associated equipment and artifacts.

Year of Formation

1963.

Number of Members

470.

Annual Fees

£15.50 UK, £20.00 Overseas.

Meetings Held

Quarterly meetings are held in Manchester and informal monthly meetings are held in London.

Publications

The society's journal is published monthly. The 40 page A4 journal has details of new issues, illustrated articles and members ads.

The society have also published various guides and checklists in the past.

PLEASE MENTION HOOLE'S GUIDE
TO BRITISH COLLECTING CLUBS WHEN
WRITING TO A CLUB

TRAVELLING POST OFFICE AND SEAPOST SOCIETY

Address 41 Paxton Gardens, Woodham, Woking, Surrey GU21 5TS

Items Collected Travelling Post Office (Railway) and Maritime Postal Material.

Year of Formation 1938.

Number of Members 240.

Annual Fees £10.00.

Meetings Held Meetings are held in London and Bristol.

Publications A quarterly journal is published. The society have also published "TPO Postmarks of Great Britain 1962–1990".

REMEMBER
ALWAYS ENCLOSE A S.A.E. WHEN
WRITING TO A COLLECTING CLUB

TRIX TWIN RAILWAYS COLLECTORS ASSOCIATION

Address 36 Sixth Cross Road, Twickenham TW2 5PB

Items Collected Trix Twin Railways, Trix Express and Trix "OO" Gauge Trains 1935–1972.

Year of Formation 1974.

Number of Members 350.

Annual Fees £10.00.

Meetings Held AGM held in Birmingham in November and up to 6 regional meetings are held.

Publications A gazette is produced quarterly. The well produced magazine has articles, news of meetings, illustrations and adverts.

The society also have a large amount of spare parts available to members.

UNITED NATIONS
STUDY GROUP

Address 86 Liverpool Road, Ashton in Makerfield, Wigan WN4 9LP

Items Collected UN, League of Nations and UN agencies philatelic material.

Year of Formation 1968.

Number of Members 100.

Annual Fees £6.50.

Meetings Held The group hold two meetings a year.

Publications The group publish a bulletin 6 times a year. The magazine contains articles, details of new issues and society news and views.

WADE COLLECTORS CLUB

Address   14 Windsor Road, Selston,
                         Nottingham NG16 6JJ

Items Collected   Wade Porcelain.

Year of Formation   1989.

Number of Members   600.

Annual Fees   £5.00.

Meetings Held   None.

Publications   The club publish a newsletter quarterly. The newsletter has details of new issues, articles and members letters and adverts.

PLEASE MENTION HOOLE'S GUIDE
TO BRITISH COLLECTING CLUBS WHEN
WRITING TO A CLUB

THE WRITING EQUIPMENT SOCIETY

Address   4 Greystones Grange Crescent, Sheffield, South Yorkshire S11 7JL

Items Collected   All writing instruments and accessories.

Year of Formation 1980.

Number of Members 500.

Annual Fees   £13.00.

Meetings Held   The society hold 5 or 6 meetings a year.

Publications   The society publish a journal 3 times a year.

REMEMBER
ALWAYS ENCLOSE A S.A.E. WHEN
WRITING TO A COLLECTING CLUB

INDEX

INDEX

There are several local collecting groups, especially for postcards and stamps, in Britain. Your local library should be able to put you in touch with such groups in your area.